The Dog with the Flute in its Mouth

萍梦美爱红家

poems by

Emily Anna King

锡萍芳

Finishing Line Press
Georgetown, Kentucky

The Dog with the Flute in its Mouth

萍梦美爱红家

Copyright © 2024 by Emily Anna King 锡萍芳
ISBN 979-8-88838-750-4 First Edition
All rights reserved under International and Pan-American Copyright Conventions. No part of this book may be reproduced in any manner whatsoever without written permission from the publisher, except in the case of brief quotations embodied in critical articles and reviews.

ACKNOWLEDGMENTS

Previously Published:
一期一会 (Cork Words 3 edited by Patricia Looney)

Thank you to my parents, friends, mentors and everyone who has become family throughout my life. I cannot express enough gratitude for your love, your support and all of the times you've made me feel joy and feel cared for and feel capable of achieving more than I thought ever could. There are so many moments that come to mind regarding how this book came to life from my mom and dad reading to me each night as a child and raising me to become who I am, my friends (Taylor, Emma, Liv, Sam and others) and our adventures through our hometowns, through Cork Ireland and beyond to my mentors and thesis advisor (Liz Quirke) working through lines and concepts and ideas with me, my high school and college communities helping to shape me, all of the journeys to embrace who I am and am becoming. I think of sunsets and late nights writing, phone calls with friends far away, and time learning a city like the shape of a lifeline. I think of many cups of tea shared with others. I think of everyone who has ever impacted my life and helped me become more me. I think of you holding this story, that is now yours, too.

I am so very grateful.

Thank you all, with everything I have.

Publisher: Leah Huete de Maines
Editor: Christen Kincaid
Cover Art and Design: Karen Burke
Author Photo: Emily Anna King 锡萍芳
Cover Design: Elizabeth Maines McCleavy

Order online: www.finishinglinepress.com
also available on amazon.com

Author inquiries and mail orders:
Finishing Line Press
PO Box 1626
Georgetown, Kentucky 40324
USA

Contents

Before 以前 1

The Story of 萍 5

The Story of 梦 11

The Story of 美 19

The Story of 爱 27

The Story of 红 37

The Story of 家 41

Ours 我们的故事 54

Translations 翻译 65

每一个蝴蝶都是从前的一朵花的鬼魂，回来寻找它自己。

Each butterfly is the ghost-soul of a flower from a past life, returning to find itself.

Eileen Chang

from west or east

first of the young rice in

the sound of the wind

Bashō

Introduction

The Dog with the Flute in its Mouth, negotiates heritage, identity and the delicate balance between the tangible and intangible elements of these spaces.

I do not know my birthday. I was found in front of a hospital. Moments before this, my life began, but the sparks of memory of this reality take a shape and then blink away before words can trace them, similarly to public records that were not permitted to exist. What remained was a collision of emotions so heavy, I could not form the words for many years of my life to describe my experience. I know now the heaviness was a love so deep, no words could do the aching emotion justice.

From 1980 to 2016, China introduced the One Child Policy as an effort to prevent overpopulation and complications associated with it. Under this law, families were not allowed to have more that one child. Due to influences from cultural values as well as strict enforcement, hundreds of thousands of families gave up children, primarily girls. It is a complex history, blood-stained and hidden, often simplified by outside lenses dehumanizing the situation through words such as "abandonment." This type of language latched to the history shrouded so deeply into the shadows that others often mistook the darkness as nothingness.

The process of writing this collection taught me that the experience of looking inward can lead to a reflection that takes on a life of its own. My heritage became not only an aspect of my story originating from my past, but also the threads of my own active creation. This collection takes influence from my cultural heritage, my lived heritage from personal experience and my literary heritage.

While the roots of my collection are deeply personal, the collection holds many different parts of me culminating in mythical space meant for myself and for the reader. In East Asian cultures, there is a story of the red thread which represents the idea that people who are meant to be together are connected by a red thread. This thread becomes an active symbol of my collection holding the work together in a unique logic, as well as representing connection within stories and beyond the pages to the reader.

Those threads also connect the aspects of my heritage tied between the East and West. While my origins began in China, I grew up in America but had incredible influence from Ireland in my creative journey. This collection holds the people who are important to me and honors the skills I've learned from a diverse cannon of authors such as Eileen Chang, Bashō, Shangyang Fang, Roberto Bolaño, Markus Zusak and many others.

From the beginning of my process, I knew I wanted this to be the most personal collection I've achieved this far in my writing journey. In order to chase my ambitions, I knew I would need to incorporate skills I've gained from studying all of the genres and other mediums. My collection harbors aspects of memoir, fiction, poetry and additional forms of storytelling such as music.

Structurally, the collection incorporates free form poetry, lyrical stanza, prose poetry, thoughtful use couplets and tercets to mirror relationships, translation and extensive use of both metaphor, simile and imagery unique to my self-created origin myth. Each word, punctuation mark and decision regarding white space and symbolic separation between stanzas and episodes carries a careful deliberation. The translation page also includes the deliberate choice to omit pronunciation to honor my own existential experience of knowing information exists, but not being able to find it right before my eyes.

The collection is meant to be read at a slow pace allowing the threads of story to build, combine and overlap like fragments of memory until they create a mosaic that is alive and unraveling before the reader. My piano teacher taught me that music is the art of time. I believe the nature of my collection with its dreamlike, imaginative logic that folds over and over requires the same consideration as a musical piece.

The collection follows a narrative and episodic structure that still leaves room for individual experiences within each poem. The core thread ties the narrator, the dog with the flute in its mouth, the child, and the stories of 萍, 梦, 美, 爱, 红 and 家 together. The narrator comes across the child who is searching for his name. The narrator offers to share the stories 萍, 梦, 美, 爱, 红 and 家 to help the child on this journey as the dog bears witness. While 萍, 梦, 美, 爱, 红 and 家 can easily represent other characters carrying their own individual stories that encapsulate aesthetics of different emotions, dynamics of loss and love and other aspects, they also carry specific meanings in Chinese. These meanings define the aesthetics, philosophical explorations and core identity of the collection. The dynamics of loss, dreamlike natures, beauty, love, the red thread referring back to the traditional East Asian myth of the red thread and family coming together in both sections of the collection and undercurrents of each poem give this collection an identity of its own.

The order of episodes carries an essential importance to the life of this collection which builds to my personal understanding of family, identity and heritage. For example, 萍 is a type of rootless water plant that represents wandering and traveling. It is also a character within my own Chinese name. This dynamic of rootless wandering defines my own beginnings as well as the opening aesthetic of the collection. 梦 stands for dream and the surreal nature of dreams defined my original understanding of my own origin. Building upon dream follows 美 beauty, 爱 love, 红 red thread and 家 family and the ethereal nature of these concepts.

The tumbling metaphors and symbols include prominent choices such duckweed, jade, kingfishers, salt and thread which connect each story to one another until they take on a universal human quality, transcending the physical reality. In the end, "everything returns to the sea" (29). Other examples of symbolic dynamics include the duckweed and red thread serving as contrasting objects that help connect a family. Salt refers to the unifying bridge of the sea between the East and West as well as a connection to healing, grief, love and joy as seen in tears which can take on multiple emotional contexts. The kingfisher represents a sense of freedom and connection between land and sea as well as a sense of wonder to me as I've yet to witness one in person. Each symbol and each image woven together to make emotion tangible is a mark of my own sense of identity. Many of the images and storylines create a sense of the ethereal, the temporary and a mythical space somewhere between reality and imagination. For me, that is the space of becoming. As these symbols return, the context and emotional echos of previous appearances echo through the reader's experience and take on new life.

Each section explores episodes jumping between Western influences, East Asian influences and individual scenes between the narrator, the child and the dog. The episodes incorporate instruments that lead to the final chapter of the collection. In the final moments, the sound of the instruments creating music together become the child's name and represent a thread of stories that combine into one. In the end, the child, the dog and the narrator are family and their heritage is the stories they share and the stories they create together. At the same time, the collection invites the reader to become a part of this myth and feel empowered to reconsider the power of their own inherited and created heritage.

The Chinese characters marking each section as well as the names of the children we cannot know referenced in the opening poem, serve as a bridge between the literal and intangible worlds where I often feel most comfortable doing poetic work. The characters may serve as concrete concepts such as family or the color red, but they also bleed into metaphor, symbol and nuanced aesthetics important for the collection. Whether it be the siblings in 梦 or the friends in 爱, the relationships formed within the stories capture the intricacy of emotion, humanness and the many aspects of my own experience with understanding identity, heritage and existence. The collection is influenced by real and created aspects of my life that take on a life of their own on the page. My story becomes a myth of its own.

The child and the Dog with the Flute in its Mouth also carry important roles in the collection. In the beginning of my process, there was not a child or a dog, but both characters emerged through an exercise of handwriting freely in the first month of working on the collection. These characters reminded me of my child self and the dogs that I've grown up with throughout my life as well as the powerful bond we shared despite not sharing the same language. The child also represents a life never lived or a life left behind in the process of a different reality unfolding. Both carry an innocence and wisdom more difficult to access as an adult, as well as an ethereal beauty contrasting a sense of infinite and deep love from their essences that carry over to the important aspect of my collection that balances heavier emotions with brightness and positive connotations. These characters carried me through the collection allowing what used to be an individual personal journey feel accompanied.

In regards to craft, my collection showcases my connection to East Asian language and literature as well as other unique influences. Besides Chinese characters used in the collection, my approach to learning Chinese also shapes my use of English. Chinese is a pictographic language where images of a word's meaning may be glimpsed through the printed character. It's drawn my focus to think about how I understand words and language. Similarly, when I think of words, regardless of language, my mind's eye conjures colors, textures and images in vivid and dynamic ways. Because of this relationship with words, when I construct a phrase, sentences or stanza, I often describe an idea based on the associated image that comes along with the word itself.

For example, in the lines, *"there is a love so lonely, / it clings like bone to rust"* (15), the imagery of loneliness and aesthetic of loneliness presents itself with sourness, rust and a core human aspect captured in bone. In this way, words are very much alive for me and live in a dynamic, pictographic, all immersive presentation that I hope to share with my reader.

In addition to the pictographic nature of Chinese, poetry and other classics celebrated in East Asia generally carry a very different aesthetic from Western pieces. East Asian work hails from a completely different history of culture, philosophy, religion, etc. It often aims for subtleties and beauty connected to sharp and specific images to capture a mood, message or intent. For example, the impermanent nature of the cherry blossom or the slight breeze through a silk sleeve under a fading moon could serve as a powerful image in East Asian work relating to philosophies and aesthetics such as Wabi-Sabi or Mono No Aware which embrace beauty in transience and imperfection (Prusinski 1). From my own experience, Western Poetry may incorporate more of a narrative form explaining more action to the reader centered around a main character or idea. It may feature an enactor upon the environment. In contrast, East Asian poetry often focuses on the environment's impact on the individual or how the individual person or situation enacts on the larger stage of the world and how they come together. While the poetry from both sides of the world may address similar topics, their presentation, level of restraint and boldness diverges into unique logic or otherworldly styles of presentation which greatly influences their engagement with the world (Lee 16). My combination of both imagistic, surrealist and the natural merged into narrative and episodic structures honor both of these heritages.

By the end of the collection, the language I share with the reader, becomes theirs. It makes home in the myth and it is something given. While this collection has carried the reader from rural to urban, ocean to surrealist spaces, to an apartment with my best friends, to my family, to scenes that encapsulate the great love I know in my own life, I hope that the reader also sees their own reflection in the work. I hope they see the places they've been, the people they care about, the emotions that connect all of us as human beings, as people worthy of love and understanding.

This is the first time I've written a collection of this size and coherence. It's been an incredible experience working with Professor Liz Quirke to create my origin story and put myself into words in a way that truly feels like me. I am endlessly grateful for this opportunity also your time spent with my work.

以前

before

four petals swirl around themselves

in water cut from light

shape of flower ink and dog tail

心

meaning heart

and the closeness of cotton and jade

fresh like lime and duckweed

a child's laughter breaking the surface of water

three friends on a log and a dog lost at sea

will you help me

help me know my name

夜里

that night,

   the moon emerged like sea glass washed in rice stones
fragments of memory   jagged silk
    lantern-shell of crab

  child crouched by an unsung sea

   waves reached for him

child far and   alone

  i reached him

☽

i found the child who brushed water-color into waves
   his face the shape of the sea
   cotton clothes loose over his frame
    pale like the petals on my wrist

☽

i love a child who asked me
  will you be my family
  will you help me know my name

   i am lost

☽

i said,
there's a song my old friend plays on the flute,
  and it sounds like windblown things—

   take my hand and we'll make our way home
   home holds the stories left behind, loved

This is the song of the children; how i cannot know their names:

萍　　梦　　美　　爱　　红　　家

take them and shield them, hold them as they cling and
lean into cotton warmth and ask
are you like me　　　　*are you like me*

do i tell a child, do i tell them
they do not exist

and if so,　　　how
how do i tell a child

　　　　　　they do not exist

irises flecked like peach blossom, shivering like hummingbird call
　　　and golden light to violet

i learned a new word:
dream
　　　is this what a dream is like?

i have no words for the unmarred softness of their skin
salted corners of their eyes

　　　lightness of a voice like sun-dried jade

i take them in my arms, i tell them

yes,　　it's like, it's like—

the moment　　before someone

calls you

　　　　home

3

回来

tonight,

the child   takes one bud in his hands
shows me the fresh green skin

asks   *will this show us the way?*

like seven scales, seven scrolls,
delicate and damp with ink

i say   *split the edge with your nail and the un-bloomed petals will know*

◐

one memory becomes a thousand, a thread

    maybe it is spring,

        or another season of melting

a place of return

◐

the dog with the flute in its mouth bears witness

    to all the things un-done

◐

come, i will tell you the stories

萍   梦   美   爱   红   家

This is the story of

萍

Ping   duckweed, wandering, traveling

> *there is a love left rootless,*
>
> *with pangs that ripple through water*
>
> *crossing the sea*
>
> *each shade of the horizon*
>
> *caught in the teeth of tears*
>
> *hope; the salve and wound*
>
> *thawed into dream*
>
> *clinging to skin*
>
> *like wet petals over sun paper*
>
> *fingertip to tiny cheek*
>
> *dimple left behind*
>
> *to be born is a memory held*

—

pond waves beyond alley
        discarded rice
        flickering bulbs on a neon sign

come home to a warm meal,   come home

woman and child weave past store fronts
quiet threads of sound
        fraying on the backs of her hands
        glass cracks in the distance

small fist in neck   of cotton shirt,
        small body in blankets
        close to chest

cold rain shimmers against streetlights
and the faint smell of oil and soy
        faint hue of ash in eyes of stone guardians
        silver flash like needle through cloud

wings of a phoenix beating in place of a dragon's roar

        rain on the steps of a hospital

lips press to forehead,
fingers brushing cheek
        sound the soft rush of stitch and sand
slow breath rising   and falling
        an ache in the wind   sweet like dried honey, breaking

hand /   unlatch

                                    no words for a love made of music

二

open door and a rush of steps   hushed voices
              child to light,   *safe*

woman's body into shadow   and the curve of a full moon,
petals against pavement like piano keys scattered in milk

the color of a first cry of birth, raw like the currents of 太湖 lake
woman carried to the sea, the water takes her, away like goodbye

    my child, you are safe now

sound of distance dressing her in silk, royal purple, red feather thread,
        pearl-lace and ash,

blown by the broken hues of a sunset,
      waves cut from a laughter pure,
           silver currents through sleeves of silk,

minnows shape the child's fate as one meant to be found
         tracing the face of the ocean reflected in a far tide

woven into water,
     into legend

one face and all of the unnamable things that we are—

      人   孩子   母亲   朋友   梦

   one song written in the tides   *she sings, she sings*

    fall into the arms of a child,
    let their salt tears keep you,
       warm like river stone
       light in their eyes

          is this what a dream is like?

                the making of a sound, the closing of distance, the thread between

☰

harvest water clear
wandering dreams submerge green
pail half filled with light

*

two hands together
lifelines pressed against the tides
glass marks left behind

*

small town festival
gems into a dragon's mouth
red bean paste to tongue

*

child born to love
family standing in pond
catfish pearls found

*

step into the tides
walk along the shore with me
pearl, breath and moon

*

one silk shoe standing
scissors against lilac sky
thread pulled to arm's length

*

flowers through stone bridge
cracks winding through river dawn

two eggs and pastry

*

city lost to smoke
into lungs this breath of flame
heir of phoenix cry

*

pine path lined with sheen
tree house nails and calloused palms
hero's story told

*

lips to forehead close
woman bearing silken sleeves
shell of streetlight glow

*

fate lined salt crystal
sound of music, shape of name
come home, come home,   please

生

gilded

leaves touch like salt-light against the skin
residue memory
three sand grains away from erasure

ghost-shape of a dimple

all the colors of a sunset pale in the palm of a hand
a wish that death is a short burst of sounds from the mouth

fading sensation of the body
in another space,

a memory of each silhouette
origin
no flesh, no bone, no blood
simple hush of tide
wag of a dog's tail

tear of fresh jade from a duckweed pond

a mouth that dreamed the sounds for

"birth"

This is the story of

梦

Meng   the farther a journey from memory, the closer it falls to dream

there is a love so lonely,

       it clings like bone to rust

low trembling voice of the cello

       delicate beauty in the long sound of

            ache—

small sugar-cracked berry to mouth

       a note unnamed

       bitter / sweet smoke like winter honey

            voice to trembling strings

—

world submerged in ice, soft desolation
like feathers between bones   and barren branch

footprints left behind, crunch beneath bare skin
outline them and ice will melt in spiral divots of fingerprints

> *only part of you*
>   *that belongs to you*

until each curve becomes a river, gleaning like jade cutting blade
bird's cry   a piccolo, pressed against the throat of wind
      the piercing edge of nightfall

❄

humans don't leave much of themselves behind
but red winter berries catch their tears
smudged in cranberry ink and snow
cold desire to make a mark on this world

                              as if it matters

❄

two pairs of red mittens say

                              it matters

cheeks blush against powdered snow
      while the bones are young
      and the throat of wind opens free

ice fractals cling to bare threads hiding pinkish hands
two small bodies giggle and ride on a wooden sled
      gem-snow dusted dog chasing behind
      feathered branch in its mouth

down a hill in the wandering paths
of autumn leaves   cherry blossoms   maple seeds

❄

trace their footprints and know duckweed, rootless
touch their fingertips and you won't exist, alone

❄

downriver, the children play under a barren branch
      smiles crack the skin of lips
        as laughter escapes

❄

memorize the shape of a winter
      and feel warmth inherent
          to all four seasons
      and the wingbeat of a heart

making the cracks of a world submerged in ice

                                  glean through thread

一

onion lamp on a front porch, street of pine and colonials
violets settle on rocking chair, umbrellas lean by welcome mat

grains of sand blow beneath front door, water bowl falls to the side
beneath golden windows, family portrait, speckled orchid

glasswork on a fireplace, baseball by the cello
dog-earred pages, covers primary colors

      made of dust and   closure

kingfisher wings spread on a glass table
polaroid gloss and ink breaking water on page

feathered sapphire and topaz
beak the needle of a compass

small hands and bigger hands
弟弟 / 姐姐
      stretch across a drawn horizon

sister tells little brother that jumping in the reflection of a puddle
allows someone to touch the surface of a world opposite

twirl on the surface of duckweed flecks, streetlights upside down
and the rim of crystalline colors blurring into bell chime

maple leaves bleed into red and gold across a face of green leaf

do people there walk upside down
do they have my favorite ice cream flavor
if i go there, will i feel better
do the people there stay or   leave   eachother

bedroom ceiling lit with stars, fragile
blue eyes stare from behind fluffy blankets
and an army of stuffed animals

cotton wings and marbled fur peek out from beneath his chin

sister tells little brother she'll read one more story before bed
as long as he pretends to sleep when their parents
                        come home

all is well   *all is well*

~~~

sister thinks, how lovely it feels to be needed

they sit beside one another under the blankets
hold a flashlight to the pages where the kingfisher
glides across a bridge of water

mirror of another world beneath
catfish whiskers and sun-lined fins

~~~

bathroom sink stained with yellow mucus
speckles of blood
        fragments of his broken lungs

~~~

little brother says,

can i say i've seen a kingfisher
if i've never touched one

if i've never stood on the banks of the water
became a bird

~~~

sister thinks,

sometimes imagination is cruel / a paradox
close like light on skin, ash and stardust caught in vocal chords
        trembling ache of sound
        and then   and then

what does it sound like when they strike the water
what does it sound like when they emerge

would it be like the softest cymbals
we've ever heard

        i hope so

two children take one breath
        and then another
until they fall asleep
the light still on

dream of blue and orange

wings of their own

三

Broken Home
Can You Fix it
Call 143-2022
   scribbles in margins of sheet music
   black and white flooring in kitchen

houseplant blooms
blood-speckled orchid, tear drop root
room flickers under dying light
   fearing silence

where the seats do not shift from their places
where sister does not eat her dinner
where the man and the woman do not look long enough
to know the color of the eyes across from them because

they are gone with two car engines disappearing down the road
with voices the color of raspberry and bruises
   leaving a kitchen soured

♩

memory two pairs of red mittens, threads sewn through
snowflake fractals
the smell of old maple from grandfather's cello, hot chocolate
    keep your hands warm
and the ache in his bones that filled the sound,
a laugh tired from its own joy
curled around notes that sung of an ebony turned gold,
   like the first summer met without tears
   low rumbling to leap of a cry,
   a smile that made a minor key out of the moon

made the girl hold the dog in hands that smelled of bone-dug holes
and upturned sunflowers, fragments of yellow,

   in a summer from before
she played her first piece on the cello
and little brother said *again, again*

♩

as the sun rises once more, the orchid repotted
        sister shifts in her seat in the kitchen
        her parents sit warmed by radio fuzz in the living room
        she picks up her bow and pencil
        smiles at the photos of grandfather and little brother
        and writes in the margins with her violet-stained will to live:

Home is Fixed
No need to call 143-2022
Thank You For Your Help

♩

the world she writes into sound and air depends upon two sides of a bridge
        made of red thread and salt gossamer

far away from home, so far they were closer than they've ever been
on the other side
        sweet mirror and the taste of lotus stem and duckweed

        through the pull of her bow, she prays that little brother is safe
            wings against water, like a kingfisher, like a dream

she plays,   she plays   and they are together

until their legs give out in one cramp blooming with heat
until their sneakers tear ragged against each shard of sun
        each cloud folded upward in the sky

        they'll save someone before dinnertime,
        before a plate fills itself with mashed potatoes,
        chicken and peas mixed with soy sauce

        as the dog pulls maple branches into the living room
        feathered like phoenix tail and dragon mouth

        a bow of his own

The Story of

美

Mei   beauty, ethereal like first love chosen

there is a love that tastes like dream-water

    new lotus and palms against meadow

and in the space between whisper and breath

    harmony blossoms like honey to spoon

notes falling bell-soft, petals to bone, water to jade

    clear song from throats of birds

        silhouette sheen

           recognition in edges of mirror

        the orange call of kingfisher

—

    before time, there was a needle that faded like bone

    it made the horizon, then fell to sand

    it told time through a moon-sliver of shade

    young love fell beyond noon in the shadow of a blade

a young woman and a young man chewed on the sounds of the city
and held small pieces like petals between their teeth, staining magenta

they sipped foam from lattes, traced ivy stems through threads of a lace fence
watched petals brush between the thorns, chips of light within the eye, sea glass between stone

they sat in a garden made of stem and crystalized ink
wildflowers painted like smoke,
nature breaking between the cracks   they talked about a future, futile

love young   love young cracks like fresh paint on the corner of a fingernail

he liked the way his hands fit in the curve of her waist
she liked the idea of someone leaving pearl dust shimmering in her wounds
    he said they'd visit the ocean, she said yes
    he said she was funny and sweet and that he wanted to hear her stories
    she told them
        he half listened and it made her smile

    they were young; love wasn't bone-brine sacrifice

a young woman and a young man stepped over sidewalk cracks
and pointed to graffiti on the side of a brick apartment building:

    one kingfisher closing it's beak around the plastic rings of soda packaging
    wings flicking water onto spray painted initials
    which would stay together under a crest of orange-feathers
    until the rain lashed the color away, corners peeling

he liked the sound of her voice soft around the vowels in his name
she liked the sound of his footsteps beside her
  he felt he hadn't seen half the world
  and started most of his sentences with "i"
she wanted to take him to her hometown, outside this city of stone dragons
  and her dreams started their confessions with "we"

the young woman and young man passed a wedding dress shop
where lace and pearl wove themselves into the shape of sea wind
until the neck swooped into the center of a wave
fabric rushed smooth towards the sleeves
  bird wings finding flight in the thread

she dreamed of a house with onion lamps and two kids after her career settled
he imagined leaving before the foundation finished

  she was young and knew their time may conclude
  like when the color of a flower deepens before death
  first in a crumpling vein and then to the edge of each petal, dry

he felt the distance he made
she pulled the sides together
  until the broken pieces looked like a door opening

the young woman and young man were not alone in the city
that swallowed softness like an oyster bathed in lemon and ice

they thought of "if" and the word resounded
in slivers of metal against windows that reached for the sky,
wind chimes and fresh herb plants,
boxes filled with pruned roses and cigarette butts,
embers fading like the tail of a phoenix

if they both had jobs in the city, they could travel in the summer
if they loved each other, they could start a family
if they made enough money, they could build a house
their house could have two kids and a dog
if they made it, they could fall asleep warm every night

if they made wishes simply,

easy love would be a possibility

                                        if the world was an easy place to be

ii.

a young woman and a young man walked over the idea of visiting the sea together
    the idea fell from their lips like a dying leaf,
      clinging to the bottom of a sandal instead of branch

they took in the sights of the city, from a foam cup fallen in puddle
to brownstone and scalloped window panes framing gossamer curtains
      and a dog blinking slow at the lemonade stand by the crosswalk

they passed the grocery store littered with candy wrappers
and chattering voices,
the low hum of harmonica
    coming from the man who performs at the corner
    of the burrito store and bank

they passed the band aid sign for the pharmacy and winding branches by the pubs

    quiet, quiet

*

they imagine their story in present tense so the loss hurts less—

they speak until they don't; they hold on until they   let go

when they separate,
the way glass scratches the corner of brick
will make her think of his shirt sleeves against her wrists

when birds collect around crumbs of pastry,
he'll think of her laugh falling in small bursts

the city will ache for them
until it adjusts to the distance   between two bodies too young
to know the people they will become,

too young to know the opening chapter stretches the longest
like the tides and the way they take and give in one soft motion,
silk sleeves in spring wind, one needle through sheen of red thread
*

after time, the kingfisher dives into the river until the catfish
grow too large to hunt
    but the path of its wings still stain the walls
like the needle in the sand that found home with a sword
    meant to slash the place where catfish become coy,

petals curl back into the palm and then back into the earth
    from two separate sides of the earth,

a young woman and a young man point to a needle-bone horizon and
remember

*

red thread falls deep into the sea like the echo of a story
melting into love and ache
so similar
    sunrise can see its face in the shape of a sunset
    poured into the ocean

iii.

    this city by the sea serves rice in conch shells, gelato with chocolate flavored pebbles and edible glitter. the city by the sea has buildings painted in pastels and sunrises that erase the cracks along windowsills. Flower boxes carry peonies and roses and restaurant fragrances of ginger, oil and garlic.

    the women wear dresses made from sea foam and the men dye their shirts colors like the underside of mussel. children pass with pigtails and plastic pails. restaurants of glass offer sandboxes for children to play in as guests swallow oysters and talk about the tides, sand-cut skin from the tides, if the city will drown under cigarette smoke.

    in the mornings, jade dragons emerge from the alleyways and step between broken glass brown and green. leftover burger wrappers slide between cracks in the concrete, plastic straws find home in the mouths of crows. dress shoes walk between beer stains and disillusioned evidence of a good time.

    in the afternoon, the streets are filled not with scraps but people smiling, laughing, yelling, pushing their way through the salted tear-currents of others. other jackets, other caramel burnt dreams, their lives and fingers stained with smoke and chipped pearl. store fronts present wedding dresses made of lace, discount summer needs, crabshell watches, perfume in clam bottles, salmon sushi and driftwood covers of novels. *The Kingfisher. Nights on the Dunes. Murder Made of Pearl.*

    at night, the city blinks awake with neon lights, alcohol stained lips and slurred words. music leaks from nightclubs, a steady bass and bodies swaying like seaweed in a tidepool. oil sheen of ocean rubbed into exposed skin, lipstick, water and barnacle, cry of a gull, and the insistence of youth caught under darkness all soaring glory and patience only a night can provide. taste of calamari and pizza. stories left for a lifetime pressed dry under moon shard.

    this city takes a bottles edge and batters it with shell and broken rock until it smooths into treasure passersby wish to take home.

    home to kitchen filled with black and white tile, ceiling with glowing stars, family room with jade lamps and board games, piano in the room beside the front door, fresh daisies in glass.

if you've been there, you'll remember the girl that plays music on the corner. you'll remember the dogs and fresh chips, the barber shops that smell like peaches and evergreen. you'll know the kindness of the people who ask if you need help, the students in their uniforms, the fresh food stalls with strawberries, glasswork and fresh coats of paint on a family portrait.

some people imagine the cobbled streets as the high tide of their life becomes a main character. others live to die. and even more walk the streets imagining an idea tucked away behind the lights that stretch across bridges, stretch across lifelines, stretch across one corner of the mouth to another in the shape of a smile.

some people fall in love in the city. some people lose love. many fall in between.
and yet, the city goes on and on and on—

    this city carries the river.
    river carries mattresses, papers, people.
        light of the moon   back towards the sea—

if you look close enough to each ripple of water,

you'll understand the flight path of kingfishers,

    the flight path of gulls.

in the end, everything returns to the sea.

This is the story of

爱

Ai   love, an unnamable thing

there is a love that heals like seawater

    it clings to wound like sand

and in the space between words said and words swallowed

    there is a wingbeat of heart

the beginning of a sweet laugh all air and then sound

    sound nameless but for

love line outlined in red thread

      shared between family and friends

            what cannot be bitter   or lost

一期一会

       They didn't make it to the sea—not all together, not all at once,

three silhouettes on sun-stripped log facing a bone-needle horizon,

lifeline made of space between light and water   skin of peach against palm

three silhouettes dance in the waves, their laughter the sounds of water over stones and shells,
tossed   salted   glimmering

sand thrown by feet soaring into the air, one great
       leap as bodies curl around themselves in laughter

❧

laughter   the only pain they ever wanted,
        only pain that bloomed into a desired place of return

caught like petals between the teeth staining them pearl and magenta

❧

one silhouette says *i knew we'd make it*
       another asks if they *remember the story of the lost dog*
            with a flute in its mouth
                a final voice says *in the end everything returns to the sea*

❧

they watch the tides long enough to decide the sound of them
may only be understood
               in the silence after,

the gentle rings of sea foam clutching each grain of sand,
bitter plum against the tongue,
like ice cream in paper wrapping melting on the corners of mouths

❧

do you remember the tea spilled on the kitchen table
        i remember the salt water river outside the window
                and the coke bottle left empty by the couch
                      sound of the dog, sound of a joke cracking a funny bone

three friends sit before the glass window
bank overlooking the river winding into a city
made of cigarette smoke, flowers woven from ivy, pastel paint

❧

on slow days,

one rises at low tide,
        one at high tide,
                one when the moon was brightest against clouds of weed
                          drifting by the balcony

❧

sometimes they speak of birds
the way they cried, the way they fell,
        the way they broke   water
as their wings shivered like new laughter:

how high do you think they can go
        they must feel most alive the moment before
                they pierce water, their wings open

is that what's it's like to feel free, caught between breath in and breath out,

        mud and light, beak and bone, brine   all weightless suspension

❧

they fall into silence on the broken sofa

shoulder to shoulder

one pair of glasses, one baseball cap, one ponytail,

each wonders:
will you remember me

until the threads of thought dissipate into sea glass,
acoustic sounds and the occasional feeling that being young was
       no longer a state of mind, but a place to be

made by small hands and impending nostalgia,
cookie crumbs left of the table
       and one more episode of an old show,
       one more song from the album

       three friends cut from a silhouette of the sea

早上

This is an important question.
What?
How do you like your eggs? Like this?
Yes! That's perfect. Almost undercooked.

✳

three friends in the kitchen
golden light and tea water steam

      until one friend leaves, to sleep

✳

two friends making eggs together
one cracks, one mixes

they add milk and butter
turn the stove on medium and stir

✳

he says   *Did you know I play the guitar?*
she says   *Did you know I play the piano?*

✳

two
friends

side by
      side

✳

she tells him about her scar, carved out by sea glass bottles
left in the city with the best view of the stone dragons   above

    scar a map of the city—

path of magenta fragments, stray phoenix beak reflected,
shooting sliver in sky, a needle through raindrop

        amber rosin and cherry blossoms into a string of pearl
            around the neck of nostalgia

the cry of gulls a classic song,
        a classic song they sing together in the color of blue

✳

she imagines the city cleaned, replaced with meadow and ivy, rice-moon petals peeking through stone bridges

    she imagines gutters made into the hollow of a flute worthy of the dog

he imagines her with him until the broken couch fades in the iris of the sunset

    sun unbruised by his fist

    their lips still in the shape of the story
    about two children in a meadow from long ago
        the story of their branch-cut sword
            saving the days they can't count

✳

two bowls of eggs, two bites

warm, black tea   comfort

花瓣

mud soaks into the wounds

you are my friend
you are my best friend

one hand passes the needle
       to the other; weaves the silk of their words

you are my mother, my father, my sister, my brother, my teacher, my lover, my—

❧

one hand passes the needle through fabric like a kingfisher piercing water
hunting minnow towards the light

on hand knows the contours of a scar, like amethyst charred against jade
valley made of barnacle and stone in skin over knee

the other knows the texture of scrambled egg
still latched to the corner of a lip, smiling
teeth stained with coffee and old stories where the characters are young

red thread follows the path of the old holding the young
to the young holding the old

and the tip of the needle, needle made of pearl,
skips the section where the mirror shows

dip of swan's neck, winding bodies of white flame and gold
their words over the sea resound

❧

two plates at the table become one
       the river dries

bed is filled, then made
       sheets turn cold

children climb and then cut down the tree
        to make a home that falls or burns or houses another

ink stains paper and smudges
        story slices and then numbs

salt stings wounds and then heals
        mud soaks into the depth of raw flesh

small hands cleanse themselves in seawater
        and then grow

☙

peach roses bloom between wax petals of ivy and jade

buds emerge,
        buds bloom,
petals open, stretch like a wedding gown,
        float like hair underwater,

open like a fist released

petals wilt and wither
        until their flesh deflates into damp grief
petals dry into death
        and then dust and the *after*

wind pushes their fragments away

to grow between bones   to grow between   another

变

to say goodbye is to say nothing at all
to say see you again
to say i love you

    there will be two mugs at the table   again

it may be a different table made of water instead of wood,
different mugs with new tea leaves
    but there will be two and our laughter
    our laughter will harmonize once more

some / time / else

where no one let's go from an embrace that is warm

🖐

two friends recognize each wave on water moves distinctly
no pattern remade in the constant rush of the tides
scallop shell of movement   wind against stone

some day they will recognize, they too are waves on water

🖐

mud-dried wounds make room for salt and sand
pale scars make a gossamer thread

small hands dye the thread red
small hands make a stitch across water

until the distance becomes silk
and the silk becomes worn
    and the moment feels devoid of time

rush of water over skin
a passing sun, no root for heritage

heritage a thing made rootless and wandering
    like duckweed, sea foam and fading laughter

This is the story of

红

Hong   red / thread / sun-dyed legend

                                    there is a love cut from legend

                                    like the legend of the sword

                   where children slash the point where catfish become coy

                the point where petals curl into themselves and begin again

                    green bud, like scales of dragon, tender stem and pollen

                              pearl dew tracing a love line

                                      勇敢　　勇敢　　勇敢

                  clean slash between the word for half of brave and dare

          echo of choice, a fish cry falling like smoke droplets with no air

                                          in rice-moon city

               blade to needle to thread to horizon to note to song

           passed down from silk sleeves to small hands and duckweed song

sing out now, sing out,   brave one

The Pianist—First Movement

Delicate lace beneath her collarbone / patterns like roses and thin streams of sunlight falling /
skirt like clouds of jade and dragon's breath / pluming with a gentleness to match her spirit /   free

stage / shining honey-wood / midnight-black grand piano / white keys glistening beneath gold
lights / soft but strong / ocean waves rumbling over shoulder blades and back / each note special / each sound mirroring
      light rain / beat of a wing /
      a world unknown born from beneath her fingertips

smell of coffee and red velvet dust against strings of piano—   bring out the sound and—

one boy and one girl, their hands beside each other, weaving sound as their figures lean in   *closer, closer*

*

The Pianist—Second Movement

the boy knows the feeling of bloody knuckles against the sun
the girl knows the thinness of water and the overripe flavor of
      speaking with kindness instead of honesty

until melodies seep into the stillness of the meadow—
smell of soil and hay
mixed with rain
          and long days
sun creased at the edge / an interrupted horizon sandy and dry, soft rustle of wild grass,
wind that holds the living and the dead, spindle petals bleeding lilac
      sometimes cruelty sours
      peels back like eyes the moment before shrapnel strikes,
      yellowed pages of a book
          touched, not read
          read, not understood, frayed like wisps of dandelion
she knows the cruel language of silence and the nuance of breaking breath,

but she speaks it with warmth, with the beauty of a dragonfly coming apart

if you hold my hand, we'll become a bridge   can you see it? feel it?
      prickles of grass beneath palms, soil pressed against skin
        that will stain the cotton of your shirt when we go home
it's not a metaphor. it doesn't have a greater meaning.
it cannot tell us if we are alive

                              it simply tells us: we are here

*

The Pianist—Third Movement

slur   delicate lace / meadow grass and collarbone / patterns like roses and
thin streams of sunlight falling / skirt like clouds of jade and spindle petals /
pluming with a gentleness to match
her spirit
      free

          he is there and she is away   lost, wandering

drawing out feeling of sparkling light against lips / soft but strong /
words to ocean waves / vibrato over shoulder blades and back / sloping hill
behind the tides /
each sound light rain / beat of wing / bridge across light and water

     Music is the art of time

*

The Pianist—Last Movement

the town is so tired
the girl is so alive
maple leaves ache for her, reach for her
she plays the keys

until she feels him in the sound
until her home is filled with light
until all those she loves stand with her in an open meadow

wildflower, honey and laughter

table full / east to west / seven glasses / carrying the sea
red thread beneath her fingertips / woven into sound
love is the sound of the piano falling from her fingertips
body pressed to instrument
head bowed
        sound   all color to light
        honey to tongue
        memory;   the aftertaste

This is the story of

Jia　　family; roots sewn red; roots sewn whole; under roof; under horizon; beyond the sea

> when a bird pierces water
>
> it is like duckweed to root; endless flight
>
> followed by the sound of a flute
>
> skipping through waves over the sea
>
> wisdom is warmth passed through generations
>
> like the distance closed
>
> between parent and child,　　three friends on a log,
>
> dog's jaw and a flute,　　petal and water,
> 　　　　mud and scar,　　　　laughter and air
>
> duet and legend　　pianist and piano
>
> a love known

问题

    the child brushes his fingers through the fur of the dog

    with the flute in its mouth

if a feeling is something given, can i ever call it mine

    the child wraps his arms around my waist until his hands almost touch,

    he squeezes

what is the difference between a sound and music,

music is made of sound

    his eyes do not hold color but shift like the sliver of silver on a fish tail

    breaking the surface

does this dog know the flute is not a stick, and how so

    the dog thumps its tail against the log struck by thunder and dried

does language blind us or—

    i take his hand and he looks at me, "look, love, we are almost there—"

—

Again, again   the sea

returns like a child,   like a dream

recognizing itself in a mirror made of water
a mirror of blossoming things

this is the place where we are—

again and again and again—

the child spins with his arms open to the air
and the cotton of his shirt catches the wind like blown-rain
pierced by the beak of a kingfisher
until mist shimmers golden, the color of hope in iris,
rays through open window

his feet dance through the sand at the edge of the waves
and grains are sent into the air like pollen dispersed
        ankles splashed
        dimples deep

he will know what it is to be found

        his smile is pure

*

the child dips his hands in stories and submerges his heart
i watch tears crack through my imaginings, my memories

this heritage is a thing un-done

i watch him spread his arms then pull them tight around his sides

lift his hands as though they carry a flute
make bridges

        hold my own

*

red thread is not made to mimic bloodlines
    [a common mistake]

it is dyed red   because red is an aching color
        a color that binds   a color that bleeds

like the distance between the cry of a cello
    and the sweet raining notes of a piano
        on a honey-wood stage

*

leaves in water
petals in water
tea-stained   water

*

fabric of life divides into buds
pressed into one another like sodden fragments of paper
until they mold themselves in the shape of bird wings
still, resting on seawater

    until a small thumb pierces them open
    one bud sliced to reveal each rice grain petal
    unbound

they bloom against skin, and bleed

against the tongue, they'd taste like cherry blossoms and dragonfruit

*

the child takes a piece of red thread

and ties it between the distance

the lives   friends share

    stretched across the ocean

*

simple days reveal a child playing in the waves
feet skipping like thread under needle

    hand brushing fur of the dog

    ankle deep in waves full of watercolor

*

boat set by the thunder-struck log
its oars resting on the shallowed edge
like cerulean feathers splayed to dry

*

one memory becomes a thousand

maybe it is spring,

maybe it is the breath

    before another season of melting

        a place of new return

二

When the sea before us dissolves into stone—

Stone dragons adorn maze alleys lit by lanterns and shop signs.

鸡肉，咖啡，家，蛋挞，福倒了

Night drips down scaled features, square snouts, thick eyebrows, taloned feet, eyes shaded in incense and prayer. Rain pools in dusted pavement and cheekbones as pale golden light outlines a woman's silhouette and the child clutched close to her chest.

Dark hair frames a rounded face, pale pink lips, freckle on a left cheek. She prays she is alone.

She looks out above the child's head, her body quiet through the night, along the curb, by the faded scent of family style dishes, chicken broth, cigarette smoke and ember stained resolve. her eyes reflect the perfection of a full moon and the understanding that salt water is salve.

The child turns, reaching out one delicate hand, finding home in the worn cotton of her shirt. The tenderness of the gesture pulls tears
from the stone guardians watching.

The woman holds the child closer but does not cry, does not allows the child's last sight of her be sadness. *Let me child only know the music of a gull's cry at the sight of lotus and pearl. Let my child press an ear to the conch shell, hear the sea.*

Her figure hugs the contours of the shops as she heads towards the hospital. Moonlight softens the child's rounded cheeks, rice grain dimples, small feet and pinky toe leaning to the side, fingernails like the small crescents on a butterfly wing.

She memorizes each curve, each dip, the scalloped shell of a closed eye,
 the shiver of eyelash displaced by rain,

Kiss against forehead an unnamable thing,

one bound to come again, but not in this way, not in this lifetime dragon's cry, hospital steps, glint of eyes washed by ocean wave, an open door—

*

Jade strips unraveled in the corner of memory passed down through ink petals,
glass vases, torn artery adorned in feathers and gems,
a mixture of color lost in itself devoid of time, reason, mixed in bowl of water
until the magenta petals bleed the shape of lotus

Soak the feet in herbs and animal blood

You will have a home when I am gone

Phoenix feather thread, scissors, mirror, binding cloth, silk shoes,
embroidered wings and waves

You will walk on the ocean

Small toes under biggest one, like a lotus, fold

You will hear the sound of your own child begging you to stop,
mama please 妈妈 please
I hear you, I promise I hear you and one day you will listen

Over and over, wrapped, cleaned, soaked, blisters, blood, clean, tuck, pull, press,
like a lotus   bloomed curled back into the moment before,
eternal beauty

You will understand:
Wisdom is knowing that love consists of great pain and great beauty,
constant sacrifice, constant strength

Shoes embroidered by the hands of your family to hide broken bones and
toughened skin, power of women hidden behind silk

How we bleed out to belong in this world, one day I hope you'll tell me it is enough,
that I was enough

You are a golden lotus, treasured, protected, loved

Keep your head high, one day cut the lotus from its stem, know the place of severance, taste the sharp tang of love and fresh water

*

one blade on a boudoir,
small enough to tuck into an elaborate bun,

pearls and gems petals above curling brown root,
knife hidden until blade known
sharp cut of lotus, melody of clean breakage,
blood rush made of sugar and water, echo of a child's cry

sleeves drenched through silken embroidery of a family name
sweet fragrance of spring blossoms like song of plum wine

stone dissolves into saltwater
an open door

it is enough

三

we are lost
we follow the path of the gull's cry
        all hollow notes and silhouette of sunbeam

        a wooden row boat carries us:
        the small child   who helps me with the oars
        dog by the boat-crest with his paws dangling into the water
        nose dipping towards each magenta petal

        gentle winds blow us towards the horizon

silver waves rewrite the story of three friends still sitting on the shore

*

i tell the child,

if you squint hard enough,
you'll see them still laughing on that log,
unaware of the distance
        between themselves   and this bone-needle horizon,
        between imagining what it is to be a bird   and becoming

i look to the face of the ocean and

        imagine my arms as wings tucked close to my sides
imagine the rush of the fall, facing myself in the mirror

unfurling each feather before i pierce jade floating on water
stain the tips of my feathers as they skim against salt

dive under lotus leaf and lily pads
where frogs rest and swans weave

        blink and—

open my eyes and see the face of the child, salt tipped eyelashes,
        softness in his cheeks,

feel magenta petals fall from my wrist
know that he flies on winds made of silk and pearl droplets

        red threads connecting him to a first needle before time,
        and the time far beyond

                my hand to his
                my lips to his forehead

                once more   *once more*

*

his call is a dragonfly's wing over water
his call skims my skin
      until his small hands wrap around my waist,

his touch makes silence shiver, its softness an echo of a dream of home
his touch is the sigh that follows a creaking porch that cannot break
through its bending

as i fall to my knees in the sand, brown glimpse of the dog returns as a force
stopping short of my shin, the dog greets me and the child
peeks from behind my back

our hands in the salt stained fur trimmed short, speckled like leaves in fall,
magnolia in spring, the first sign of melting

his face is the shape of the ocean
his body holds the breath of the tides

the child moves me
the child loves me

      and i pray the child knows me

should i call you 妈妈 *or* 姐姐 *or—*

i trace my name on his skin as i hold him close.

i say, there is no need to call me now.
我一直在你的身边。
i am always by your side.

it is warm, it is safe

四

the child asked me if i know the world   all i know is that the world goes on

a life unfolding like a bud split open   early   pale ink in the unborn
bloomed   light magenta   our hands overlapped in clear water
petals opened by thumbnail

leaves on waves family gathered around wooden table

minnows sift through soft whispers   *i love you*
                                                            i miss you

      on the last day, the ones who love the world most still call out
            i'll see you tomorrow   *i'll see you later i'll see you*

people will love, hate, hurt, hope take their fists and unravel them like
peach roses in glass vases in windows to the sea or the city
or the face of the dog stopping by from next door

people will float in water and become the sea, become a bird
                                                        unravel themselves

reach out with the simple hope   the simple want   that they are loved

    and to love in return

ice melts in leaves staining the water with colors, leaves falling from branches into
seeds into buds into small hands   small hands that grow into large hands
and hold another

overlap in clear water   like a life unfolding

    a music for the words that cannot stitch a silk sleeve, stitch a wing blue
    thread a horizon into language   into words

        shape of family made   the place of belonging

回答

Hold a conch shell to the ear, and you'll hear the ocean

  妈妈 said to the waiting tides,

  when you hear these stories, know that they are my presence not my absence

A voicemail crinkles the child's voice across the surface of shell, curved, pale pink and speckled

pressed to ear—

妈妈 the ocean looks like me

妈妈 i'm okay and i have friends and family and people who love me

妈妈 i met a dog

妈妈 i hope you're not sad

妈妈 i'm okay

妈妈 i'll remember your stories

妈妈 i'll share them

red threads tremble against the notes of words

  and the line ripples like a fingertip pressed to the tides, moon-glass a rippling wave

    carrying all that cannot be held—

妈妈 i know i'm loved

我们的故事

Ours

an origin story

is the moment

before the seed of the lotus

grows beneath   *cherry blossom ink*

small hands   *reach for glimmering keys*

melted ice

gentle intake of breath

a melody sung from the silver hollows of a flute

salted lips   *a moment in time*

left open

like lemon sliced   or

red thread through wishbone

颤抖的花瓣之歌

Song of Trembling Petals

      如水的镜中，你向我伸手 you reach out to me through the water mirror 轻轻触及 hand skimming 我破碎语言的残片 broken fragments of my language uncovered like slivers of sea glass among pebbled tides 粉红，剔透，漂浮着 pink, translucent, floating

      染甜了格雷伯爵茶的味道 sweetening taste of earl grey against the tongue 花瓣蜷缩着自己 petals curling into themselves 像燃烧的盐水 like charred brine cut by sunlight 镜中，我们的脸 our faces turn clear in the mirror

      紧贴着 together 两颗雀斑 two freckles 面颊光滑，如小鱼的影子 cheekbones smooth like shadow of minnow 红宝石 rubellite 颤抖的嘴唇 trembling lips 想象笑有小火花 imagining laughter and small sparks 说靠近我一点 saying come closer to me

      好在我耳边呢喃 become a whisper in my ear

      有天希望认出我们的名字 one day i hope to recognize our names 在海里，在火里 in the fire-light of the ocean 我手里汗珠 pearl of sweat in my hand 绽放 blooming
      命脉如茎 lifeline the stem

            我愿永伴你身旁
            i wish to always be by your side

      like glass echo, like nameless things,
      like a hidden reflection in trembling petals
      an ethereal love still shivering
            close

    another season of melting—

the difference between one story

                        and a thousand

The Dog with the Flute in its Mouth

The dog with the flute in its mouth knows the words for
音乐　鸡肉　同性　红线　人类　幸福

The dog with the flute in its mouth—

loves a girl with magenta petals on her wrist
        and wanders the shape of blue veins to find her

hugs the contours of pastel buildings in a city
        strewn with ivy flowers, smoke filled breath, water stem
daydreams

tail stained with mud paint over a caramel back the color of
        toast on a sunday morning   apricot jam

green fragments of bottles flash like each click of nail against pavement
        sound shatters like confetti from beer stained youth, discarded

the dog parts a jaw lined with glistening hunger
        nose a compass, for the cotton warmth of home

dish of water, a bed filled with feathers, smell of flour on chicken thighs
        basil leaves in the window,
            red threads over a basket of chocolate chip cookies

the dog is young
the dog is old

        and its love is the same

        like orchid in living room, speckled and bleeding

The girl with magenta petals on her wrist—

holds a flute before her lips

    breathes a song that echos sea-longing

pulls her breath like the tides
    in and out until the notes are air no longer

    but sesame and seaweed, salt and water

passersby wade through each note
    a feeling blunted by crumpled ash   moving bodies

torn boots, leather strings, high heels, rhinestone soles
    hitching by her figure, snap against stone

like a cry submerged or a heart beat suppressed
    by the small fist of a child

she stands on the corner between lawmaker and gelato store
    where the sun rises in silk and dissolves in night thread

    border of continent, shore of street,
    soft space between top and bottom lip

        small wind from words left untouched

            released

When the dog meets the girl   through sway of skirt obscured by man
    in the center of the street, along the yellow line dividing the pavement
into two   halves

    for the first time

    a man opens skinny arms to the light
jacket falling torn off his shoulder, spread like bird wings
to the sound of her music

        sun shrouded in cloud and the haze of urgent lives

swallowing coffee and bitter minutes
    until they drown in caffeine and sweet grains of time

    when living requires a lens and a pill
and a soul that shies from corners of the streets

        rough edges dig into the palms of personal desire
until they bleed into rust and charcoal poured into gutter

yellow teeth brown on the molars as the man's dimples etch themselves deeper
    into scent of fresh gelato from the store next to his swaying body

her notes outline a neon welcome sign and leap in time with car lights blinking
left, right before them

            the steady currents of briefcase, backpack, bouquet of flowers
from the grocery store, another man drops
                        a chicken leg
                    like charity money for the girl

inviting the dog forward,   to the place in front of the musician's feet

    in that moment she does not know if she smiles
because of him being a dog or   because of him finding a meal

the moment he wags, her notes glean like a sharpened sword
        as the sun emerges
she rocks from foot to foot as the dog memorizes the taste of honey-char and
life sustained

content, the dog learns the feeling of warmth within his belly and the shape of
magenta   petals falling from her wrist as she brings the sound of the
sea

to the man believing himself a bird

            the dog who fell in love thanks to a chicken bone

                    and a path the shape of her veins

After seven years
the girl's music flees the street corner
and the dog's ribs reach for her through tissue paper sides

reach for an old memory when—

she brought a snack of burger rind and cheese
to a warm bed
in a warm house
where they snuggled over sheets
learning to read music

the dog wanders to remember this feeling
as the river stones warm beneath the summer sun
and drunken laughter near the docks

pebbles smooth under his paws
his fur ruffled and faded, jaws dry
like petals preserved, wrinkled faces
        and staunched love

In the end

      it is a hairline fracture along the river bend, a split end, a threaded vein
      flattened by mud paws, rough steps, sand pressed

      fingerprint left behind, smudge of scar under clattering seaglass,
      puddle-mirror to living room of an   old life

glint of silver tangles itself in seaweed beneath the bridge
laps fresh water and the faint taste of salmon struggling upstream
the dog bends and wraps his jaws around the silver form
hard against the teeth, object rounded, and smooth

he lifts the shape of a flute between his jaws
remembering the wind of her music, winged tide in her smile

dripping and cold,   he doesn't let go

After the end
the dog with the flute in its mouth still
wanders the path of her veins
                      lives a song made of

音乐　鸡肉　同性　红线　人类　幸福
music, chicken, empathy, red thread, humanity, fortune

回家   *returning home*

the sea returns to the child
        the sea returns to me

the child wraps his arms around the dog
        with the flute in his mouth

the air tastes of salt, seaweed   lightness of peach and a gliding wing
waves reach for us   their movement a hush   a whisper   a dream

he asks, does the place we come from   have a sound

i tell him   the things we do not know do not change the way we love
the way we are loved   and love,

like petals swirling around a broken stem in a glass that holds the sea

              unattainable   untouchable
    as children imagine themselves racing across horizon

the dog wags his tail, splashes droplets into air
like salt from silk sleeves,   blossom open through ice

                the things that i am and we are

                                    emerge

名字

first breath—
ocean holds the sound of mother's comfort / first cry of birth /
calloused hands of father / laughter of friend /
strength of sibling / loyalty of family / red thread
an unspoken name known in the shape of music—

when springs comes, sheets of ice glisten like lemon peeled
and cracked under soft and inevitable palms, seeds fall into warmed earth,
burst into soft magenta petals that mark the skin, slender wrists

into summer, pale light becomes harsh and salt water beckons
to those who play in the sea,
wash ashore, happy, laughter fills the hollows of shell, curved twist of catfish,
empty sands in red tides, mends lost bones

fall takes leaves and dyes them into thread that falls between sidewalk cracks, scratches breeze
awakens the city to dust against long sleeves and small jackets, pollen cooled, released,
children jump in the piles of disintegrating maple, call of cold

winter frosts where dandelions used to grow, welcomes sleds and clear scent of new
between barren branches, bodies bend towards ice pools, reflections of red mittens
until spring sun emerges against iris, against piano keys

      and the four seasons are known.

each sound is a corner of the earth, a place the horizon reaches for,
    this path of life is yours and ours, known, unknown,
the taste of salt and honey, dream-water against the lips, against the tongue

*

the dog with the flute in its mouth knows the melody
of the first set of silken sleeves dropping
salt pearls to water

                    and we follow—

钢琴   短笛   大提琴   小提琴

长笛   钹   嗓音   笑声

乐队   旋律   和谐   音乐

sounds of the music,   horizon-born,
    all of the unnamable things   together

*

i tell the child   i tell myself   i tell you

            the music is the sound of your name

                    it calls us home

come,   come

it is all about to begin
        like an open door and the petals flowing between

                    开门,

                            心

—we are loved in the way we are found
        this love blooms in the place where we leave you
                            the place we are
                                    let it hold you
close

            yes,

it's like, it's like—
the moment   before someone   calls you

home

萍　　梦　　美　　爱　　红　　家

翻译　　Translations

萍　　　　duckweed

梦　　　　dream

美　　　　beauty

爱　　　　love

红　　　　red

家　　　　family

心　　　　heart

一，二，三，四，五，六，七，八，九，十
Numbers 1-10

以前　　　before

夜里　　　at night

回来　　　return

太湖　　　Taihu Lake

人　　　　person

孩子　　　child

母亲　　　mother

妈妈　　　mama

朋友　　　friend

生	to be born
弟弟	little brother
姐姐	older sister
一期一会	Japanese proverb meaning once in a lifetime meeting
早上	morning
我们的故事	our story
花瓣	flower petal
变	change
勇敢	brave
鸡肉	chicken
咖啡	coffee
蛋挞	egg tart
福倒了	fortune arrived
问题	question
回答	response
我们的故事	our story
名字	name

钢琴	piano
短笛	piccolo
大提琴	cello
小提琴	violin
长笛	flute
钹	cymbals
嗓音	voice
笑声	laughter
乐队	band
旋律	melody
和谐	harmonious
音乐	music
回家	returning home
开门	open door

感谢你

thank you

心

Works Cited

"Basho: The Complete Haiku." *The Haiku Foundation Digital Library,* https://www.thehaikufoundation.org/omeka/items/show/206.

"Great Chinese Writer Eileen Chang 张爱玲 Quotes." *Chinesetolearn,* 28 Dec. 2012, http://www.chinesetolearn.com/eileen-chang-zhang-ailing-quotes/.

Lauren, Prusinski. *Wabi-Sabi, Mono No Aware, and Ma: Tracing Traditional Japanese Aesthetics Through Japanese History.* https://castle.eiu.edu/studiesonasia/documents/seriesIV/2-Prusinkski_001.pdf.

Lee, Joseph Tse-Hei, et al. "Reflections on Literature: East and West." *Digital Commons*, Global Asia Journal , https://digitalcommons.pace.edu/cgi/viewcontent.cgi?article=1635&context=lawfaculty.

Emily Anna King (锡萍芳) is a recent alum of University College Cork's Creative Writing graduate program in Ireland. She currently teaches creative writing and English at Wilbraham and Monson Academy in Western Massachusetts.

Her most recent publications are found in *Tír na nÓg, Massachusetts Best Emerging Poets 2019* (Z Publishing), *Pamplemousse, Lily Poetry Review, Paragon Press,* and *Otherwise Engaged Journal.*

While her work often explores the Chinese American adoptee experience, she is also passionate about the intersectionality between language and music.

Besides writing, she loves spending time with family and friends, playing tennis and baking.

There is an origin story that I cannot know; it is mine.
There is an origin story that I must make; it is mine.

The Dog with the Flute in its Mouth negotiates heritage and the new life it takes on in the space of absence. The collection follows the journey of the narrator, the child and the Dog with the Flute in its Mouth as they search for the sound of a name and a way to return home. It represents a deep love that both creates and bears witness. Along their journey, they discover the stories of:

萍	Ping	duckweed, wandering, traveling
梦	Meng	dream
美	Mei	beauty
爱	Ai	love
红	Hong	red, red thread
家	Jia	family

Come home, please. Come home.

May our story become yours.

www.ingramcontent.com/pod-product-compliance
Lightning Source LLC
Chambersburg PA
CBHW020340170426
43200CB00006B/441